MW01247176

The Joy of HR

Elevating HR's Role as a *Trusted* Partner

Lotus Buckner

Balance Network Media

Published by Influence Network Media, Loveland, OH 45140.

The information in this book is provided for informational purposes only and is not intended as a substitute for the advice of professionals. The author and publisher assume no responsibility for any errors or omissions, or for any actions taken based on the information provided.

ISBN Paperback: 979-8-9883607-8-0

ISBN eBook: 979-8-9883607-7-3

Books may be purchased for educational use. For bulk order request and price schedule contact: lotus@lotusbuckner.com.

Cover Design by Michell Moy.

Acclaim for The Joy of HR

The Joy of HR is a captivating book that is an absolute must-read for senior leaders, seasoned HR veterans, and ambitious HR professionals who are ready to take their careers and organizations to the next level. Buckner is an extraordinary storyteller who blends her relatable experiences with sharp business acumen. Her five tenets provide timeless wisdom on transforming HR into a more human-centric and results-driven powerhouse. With a perfect mix of heartfelt insights and unfiltered realness, this book is guaranteed to inspire and challenge you.

Gregory Tall, The Highest Energy Facilitator You'll Ever Experience at The Gregory Tall Company

The Joy of HR is a magnificent book and a powerful reminder of the critical role that HR plays in shaping the success of any organization and its people. With stories and remarkable insights, Buckner shows how HR professionals can break free from the transactional mindset and become strategic partners who solve real business problems. The book's five tenets offer a roadmap for HR leaders to learn the business, build relationships, communicate effectively, do the right thing, and impact culture in a meaningful way. This is a must-read for anyone who wants to experience the joy of HR and make a lasting impact on people, culture, and strategy. As Buckner says in the book, "There is a special trust built when we, in HR, can help solve real business problems."

Enrique Rubio, Founder at Hacking HR

The Joy of HR is a must-read for people leaders, including HR, operations, CEOs, and founders alike. Through powerful real-life stories, Buckner takes readers on a journey of practical ways that executive teams can align the HR, talent, and culture strategies with the business and partner with their HR leaders to cultivate company success that is still people-centric. In an ever-divisive world, *The Joy of HR* reminds us of the criticality of connection at work and its impact on overall success.

Andrew Higashi, CEO & Founder at ChangeEngine

What a timely and needed book! The world of HR has gone on one heck of a journey these past years, and many do feel lost and depleted. There is a palpable need to recapture our personal why and find joy in the role again. Buckner's willingness to share her experiences in an approachable and vulnerable way is a welcomed guide.

I am particularly a fan of the joy of learning the business and building relationships. There is so much joy in *specifically* knowing how we can impact a business through a shared, respected partnership. Buckner has been able to achieve that and shares that it takes not just tip-toeing but jumping out of our comfort zones to forge that kind of experience. The rich joy of HR is found not so much in being a department but being a source of *measurable and shared* impact. Buckner has acute business acumen, so her ability to guide both HR professionals and their leadership counterparts to this place is one of the many gems of this book. The synergy of HR and operational leadership can indeed be a joy!

JoAnn Corley, Executive Advisor & Leadership Coach at Manage Global

The Joy of HR is a must read for anyone who aspires to be a strategic HR leader. Buckner makes a compelling case for why people leaders can be most impactful if they take the time to truly understand their companies and industries and not simply stay in their HR swim lane. As people management becomes more complex, this holistic understanding of pain points and opportunities can make HR leaders crucial voices on the executive team.

Raphi Savitz, Head of GTM Finance at Alegeus

The Joy of HR is a beacon for those who are looking to learn more about the dynamic world of human resources. It is a treasure trove of wisdom, distilling five fundamental principles that encapsulate Buckner's passion and dedication to the field. A recognized leader and innovator in HR, Buckner shares her insights with a blend of practicality and inspiration, making it an essential read for anyone aiming to excel in HR. Her approach is not just about policies and procedures; it's about nurturing a culture that values every individual and their contribution to the organization. Whether you're just starting out or looking to refresh your perspective, *The Joy of HR* promises to ignite a passion for HR that is both profound and infectious. Dive in and embark on a journey to discover the heart and soul of effective human resource management.

Joni Duncan, Vice President of People & Culture at Greater Chicago Food Depository

In *The Joy of HR*, Buckner coaches readers on how to join her in transforming human resources from an outdated department to one that aligns with business strategy. Through stories and lessons learned, she shares how employing psychology, along with strategic communication, to engage employees leads to better outcomes. Throughout this book, Buckner's intelligent enthusiasm and can-do attitude inspires action. Whether you are new to HR or a senior organizational leader, Buckner's inspirational narrative will help organizations become the best they can be.

Jeanan Yasiri Moe, Director of Strategic Communications and Public Affairs at Wisconsin Alumni Research Foundation (WARF)

In a landscape often fraught with challenges and uncertainty, *The Joy of HR* is a beacon of inspiration for HR professionals seeking to reignite their passion for the field. With poignant insights and actionable strategies from a storied HR leader, this book offers a roadmap for navigating the complexities of modern HR while staying true to the core values that draw people to the profession in the first place. Through engaging anecdotes and practical advice, Buckner reminds us that at the heart of HR lies the opportunity to make a purposeful impact on individuals and businesses alike. *The Joy of HR* is a rallying cry for reclaiming the joy and purpose that initially fueled our journey in HR. A must-read for anyone committed to fostering positive change and human-centric leadership in the workplace.

Allison Peschel, VP of Client Service at JB Training

The Joy of HR is full of actionable ideas of how to get the most from & for your HR team. Even in the introduction, Buckner shares a down-to-earth action that made a difference for her and her organization, that any of us can do. Invest in yourself and your team with *The Joy of HR*'s practical ideas to build up your organization, your team, and individuals. You won't be sorry.

Having collaborated with Lotus on board initiatives and special projects, I can attest that she lives & breathes what you find in this book. She finds and brings joy to the work, and she inspires others to do the same. C-suites and Board Rooms can rest assured that *The Joy of HR* will help enhance your leadership. She shares not just HR tips but everyday leadership tenets like Learning the Business and Building Relationships and Doing The Right Thing, that will make your organization stronger. Bring some Joy to your organization with *The Joy of HR*.

Emily Endert, Corporate Director of Human Resources at Covenant Woods

The Joy of HR is a timely reminder that people are, and always have been, organizations' greatest assets. The HR professional has long evolved past the "personnel department" stigma and is truly a difference maker to successful companies' bottom line. A strong combination of Buckner's multi-angle storytelling and her curated class of professional contributors make this book not only a true representation of the modern-day HR work happening around the globe but also serves as a refresher for why so many decided long ago to serve people as well as their organizations.

TJ Mercer, Senior Director of DEI North America at Experian

Contents

Foreword

Have you spent much time around little kids? They see life in an unfettered, unbiased, curious, and life-fulfilling way. They exude joy!!

Years ago, I was in a choir that toured during the summer between school years. I was a freshman in college at the time. The first church we performed at was kind enough to have a potluck dinner after the concert. My fellow choir members who were now "adults" (at least in age) went through the line to get a plate of the incredible display of food, and then they made sure to split up and sit at the various tables where other adults were seated. After I went through the line and got my plate, I spied a table that was low to the ground surrounded by equally small chairs.

The table was full of children who were giggling, playing with their food and talking about whatever came to mind. I moved over towards them and pulled up a small chair and sat with them. The look on their faces was memorable. They were shocked that an adult would come sit with them. Now, you need to know that I'm a very tall person at 6'4" so I looked especially strange trying to fit in this small chair around this small table. My knees were even with my shoulders which made the kids howl with exuberance even more. It was an amazing dinner. I joined in instantly and laughed, made jokes and listened intently to every story that was shared. I was enveloped in their world of joy.

Afterwards, my fellow choir members called a "meeting" to discuss the behavior of its members. (It was really meant to address me and I knew it.) I was chastised for not conforming and sitting with the adults who were kind enough to bring their food to share. How dare I sit with children!!! On top of that, to let the kids climb all over me and play with them was just unprofessional. When they had finished chiding me, I immediately responded, "I'd rather be surrounded with joy than become an adult like any of you." The room was silent. At the next concert, others joined me at the kid's table while the majority fell in line into the less joyous world of adulthood.

This story is reflective of today's workforce and especially the profession of human resources. We work in environments where conformity is valued far more than individuality. We support, create and revel in systems meant to confine and control others because we've allowed HR to fall into this dark rut. Thankfully, Lotus Buckner is swimming against this tide with her book on the joy we can find in practicing HR!!

She brings a realistic, tangible, and needed direction not only for the profession but also for each professional who chooses to take on the mantle of being in this vibrant field. It's been missing for so many people and this has led to a sense of dread for those who call this field their occupation. That needs to change . . . now!!

You see, the same young man who sat at the kid's table is still doing it. I too believe in living in joy and expressing a sense of gratitude in building people-centric organizations and have the 35+ years I've intentionally been in HR. When Lotus and I connected years ago, I could feel, sense, and see the joy she had in who she was and how she valued others. This was true for those in her life and in the HR roles she held in the workplace. She didn't give pep talks and hang inspirational posters around the offices. She invested in the lives of others on purpose, which led to her being wildly successful wherever she worked.

She has taken the light and life she lives daily and put it onto the pages of this incredible book. She exemplifies joy and I can feel it in a palpable way when reading every word of her book, *The Joy of HR*, and I know you will too. Join us at the kid's table and recapture the joy of working with humans. You'll be glad you did!!

Steve Browne, SHRM-SCP, Chief People Officer, LaRosa's Inc. and Author of *HR on Purpose!!*, *HR Rising!!* and *HR Unleashed!!*

Dedication

To *Shirley Abernathy*, my dear friend and colleague who passed much too soon. You believed in me when no one else did. You believed in me when I didn't even believe in myself. You believed in me when I was just an intern with no formal or professional experience to my name.

You saw my naivete. You saw my inexperience. You saw my mistakes. Yet, you saw my potential above all else. You saw *me*.

You were the first and only person in the entire company that every employee knew, loved, and shared a critical moment with – their first impression of all of us in HR.

You taught me the power of relationships, the power of reaching beyond our roles and our departments, and the power of remembering someone's name, their family members' names, and their pets' names. You taught me how to lead beyond my title, how to hold myself and others accountable with respect and dignity, how to bring joy and humor to my work, and how to tell and share time through special experiences rather than a clock.

Most people reading this will not know what this means but it is 2:00 p.m. somewhere, my dearest Shirley. I still miss you and you still inspire me. This book is for you – you believed in this book before I believed in it, before anyone believed in it.

Introduction

WHEN I THINK back on my time in HR, I remember when my company was about to launch an employee experience survey. My Chief Human Resources Officer (CHRO) at the time asked us to get 80% participation from the team. Even the third-party administrator of the survey laughed at him because it was such an unrealistic goal; far from the benchmark of what they normally see. However, I actually found his stretch-goal quite motivating.

I took this burst of motivation and called up a coworker. She was an associate in the department who knew as many, if not more, people than I did in the company. I told her about my boss' goal, and initially, she laughed. But, as I expected, she knew I was going to try and surpass the 80% participation goal our CHRO set. She also found the challenge rather exciting. So, she followed up with, "Just tell me when and where you need me."

She and I spent weeks rounding every department in the company to remind people about the survey. We learned that many people did not even know it was happening because they were too busy to check their emails regularly. We also had team members who *did not know* how to check their emails – historically, those departments just didn't get results – so we held computer lab sessions for those who needed it to come and get help.

We learned so much about every part of how the business operated. Team members were so excited to see us in their spaces for a positive reason instead of for an issue. So, they happily showed us around, told us about everything they do, demonstrated their new tech (we even got to play with robots once!), asked us for feedback about their upcoming initiatives, fed us (so many of them had treats ready for us), and enlightened us about their business and finances.

The team members across the company also asked us questions and shared their feedback about HR. We listened and acted on every item; even though most of these items had nothing to do with the employee experience survey we were promoting. See, we didn't just walk in and start telling people about the survey. Our goal was to improve the employee experience. So, we walked in and said, "How can we help?" Showing that we cared and truly wanted to help better their department was key.

Some departments took us literally and had us put on their uniforms and get to work! Those more hands-on experiences were my favorite! So much perspective, appreciation, and common ground can be gained when we have a real opportunity to put ourselves in someone else's shoes.

These first-hand experiences were one of the turning points that helped turn the reputation of our HR department around. When I was promoted, I integrated this type of relationship-building within our entire team. In fact, employees started getting excited when we would randomly show up in their departments rather than being scared or worried. They stopped running away when they saw us and started running towards us to say "Hi," to share feedback without prompting, and to ask us questions.

This new approach was only the start of many great things to come, but it is *why* I wrote this book. I have been lucky enough to experience, advise, and lead multiple HR transformations (for lack of a better word) across various industries and many companies. It made me realize what a dire need there is to transform HR departments into trusted partners, rather than them continuing to be a transactional function within a company. Don't get me wrong, many of the transactions are a necessary part of doing business, but HR is, and can/*should* be, much more than that.

I want to see HR professionals impact businesses positively, and genuinely feel the impact they are making on the business. I want to see HR professionals grow their careers within HR and beyond because their HR experience is one that is valued by all departments. I want to see HR leaders become go-to businesspeople in their companies and obtain the financial support necessary to run a strategic function. I want to see my fellow HR executives become the next Chief Operating Officer (COO) or Chief Executive Officer (CEO) of their companies.

Once I got into HR, I did not think I could get out. I thought I was stuck in an HR career forever; a career that was archaic, boring, and disrespected. I never would have thought that I would have opportunities to impact the businesses in which I worked in a positive manner, let alone be asked to run an operations function.

When COVID hit, I was working in healthcare. I remember laughing at my executive team when they asked me to build and lead a cross-functional operations team. I seriously thought it was a joke because I had no clinical background. When I realized they were serious, I jumped at the opportunity. As

I have mentioned, I am often invigorated by a good challenge.

It was not an easy ask. There was no playbook, no training, and no guidance. However, we ultimately set up a command center in less than 24 hours, redeployed 400+ employees into 8,500 open shifts utilizing their transferable skills, proactively obtained 250,000+ supplies donated at a time when donations ran dry, put in place an entrance screening strategy and team, helped launch a vaccine clinic, and much, *much* more.

My point in including that experience in healthcare is that HR leaders and professionals can do much more than traditional, stereotypical HR tasks. Gone are the days when every HR professional simply fell into their roles. It is now commonplace for colleges and universities to offer HR degrees from associates to graduate levels. However, the beauty, in my humble opinion, is that the HR profession is one of the most diverse career paths when it comes to education and work experience. Many HR professionals come to their roles with MBAs or other business degrees or with previous business and operational experience from departments other than HR.

We are now equipped to align HR strategy and business strategy. We often have large networks of cross-functional professionals from different industries. We *can* be a go-to business function. There is a lot of joy in being a part of an HR department and in working with an HR department, but it does take a lot of intentional decisions and mindset shifts.

Having supported many companies through the shift from transactional HR (think stereotypes of "paper-pushers" or "policy police") to strategic HR, I know that every company and industry has its unique needs. I've distilled the most common lessons learned that are relevant (regardless of company and industry) and shared them in this book. I have invited some people/HR leaders along the way to share their stories as well. I hope that my experiences and the experiences of these esteemed leaders will help us all create positive change for our companies. Whether we are an HR professional or leader, a business professional or leader, or an executive or CEO.

More importantly, I want to bring the joy back, or maybe introduce joy, into the profession of HR. I'm well aware that I'm writing this on the heels of a very challenging few years for the people and HR function. I've seen my peers leave the industry in droves. For those that didn't leave, they felt like changing companies would bring their joy for HR back. Except, it didn't.

One of my favorite humans, whom you've heard from in the foreword to this book and probably are very familiar with already, is Steve Browne. He is a legend in the HR space and truly the most giving person I know within the HR community. What truly makes him stand out, though, is his pure, unwavering passion for the profession. It just consumes you in the best way upon meeting him, virtually or in real life, because he exudes positivity unlike anyone else. He is a sought-after speaker, acclaimed author, inspiring father, and leads a highly respected HR team full-time. Even with his busy schedule, he makes so much time to give back to this profession that he loves so much.

In his book, *HR on Purpose*, Steve asks a question that really hits home for me. It forced me to face and think about the last several years of uphill battles that many HR professionals experienced. In fact, he wrote a whole chapter about it. The question is, "Why?"

Why did we go into HR? He encourages us, as HR employees, to think beyond the paycheck. What's our purpose?

Whenever I'm feeling down about HR, which is natural and happens from time to time, I think about Steve's question. "Why?" When things get tough or overwhelming in our work, we can feel stuck or forget why we went into this line of work in the first place. We might even lose sight of the real work we were meant to do, how to make a difference, and how to move our work and ourselves forward.

That's where *The Joy of HR* comes in. I want to share some overarching principles that will help us when we feel like we are up against a brick wall, when we feel like we cannot make positive changes because we have no buy-in, or when we feel that our department has the reputation of being a "personnel department" or "the policy police."

I'll talk about finding joy again through the five tenets that will help any leader support a more strategic HR function. I'll discuss getting out of HR, getting out of our own heads, getting out of our assumptions, getting out of our comfort zones, and getting out of the way to accomplish the most meaningful focus areas in the business.

My book is focused heavily on HR but the reality is that good HR and good leadership have similar requirements. So, anyone looking to make a positive impact in their company can benefit. My wish for this book is to serve as a source of inspiration and action to make the workplace a better place and for everyone to experience the joy of HR.

Chapter 1

The Joy of Learning the Business and Building Relationships

Get Out of HR and Our Offices

IT WAS A colorful fall day in 2013 as I drove into work. It was just a normal day of work, as far as I was concerned.

Except, it wasn't.

I was young in my Human Resources career. Just two and a half years in at my company, which was a fairly traditional place to work with incredibly tenured team members. Celebrating 40-year work anniversaries was the norm. It was a different time back then. The idea of transferring departments with my measly two and a half years of experience behind my name was looked down upon by most.

That day, though, was the day such an opportunity – transferring departments – presented itself. Destiny? Perhaps. It definitely set the course for the rest of my career.

My company was about to embark on the largest, enterprise-wide initiative of its long history. I was intrigued. I wanted to be a part of it!

Then, the phone rang. Yes, the phone *rang*. And no, not my cell phone. The phone that sat on my desk with a cord so I could only speak to the other person from the comfort of my not-so-comfortable office chair.

It was my executive leader. Why was *he* calling *me*? The nerves set in.

He began to tell me about a new initiative that would change the way our organization operated forever. I had already heard about it, but I let him finish his spiel. He asked if I wanted to work on it.

"Yes!" I exclaimed before he could even finish the question. Immediately embarrassed by my reaction, I attempted to correct it.

"I mean, how can I help?" I calmly asked. He chuckled.

"I thought you might be interested," he said, providing me some relief to, what I thought was, my overly enthusiastic initial response.

He went on to explain the role he wanted me to play in the project. He wanted me to organize and help support the recruitment process, since it would require a team of about 120 internal people. This team would be comprised of employees who would transfer to this newly designed department and be formally trained and certified to do the job.

There was an unexpected requirement though. Employees had to pass a three-part assessment to even qualify for consideration for an *interview*. The roles were all heavily technology-based and the department was part of the overall IT division.

So, I started working on my assignment. As I met with the leadership team, the vendor, and the consultants, I began losing my excitement for being a part of the project.

I quickly realized that my role would be very short lived. I would help build this team, which I loved doing by the way; but then, my job would be done.

The more I learned about this initiative, the more my desire to play a larger role grew. I wanted to really be a part of it from beginning to end.

So, I worked up the courage to reach out to both my direct supervisor and my executive leader and expressed my interest in applying for one of the 120 open positions available within the new department. While they were a little surprised by my desire to move to a completely new department doing a completely different job, they gave me their blessing to apply.

I took the exam and was sure I failed miserably but I also knew that I had nothing to lose at that point. To my surprise, I passed and was offered an interview.

Then, the day came. I was made an offer to leave a job I loved, a team I loved, and a profession I loved, and knew,...to completely change direction.

As I sat there debating my decision, I received a counteroffer to stay. I asked myself "Should I take a promotion in HR or go to IT?" The safe bet was surely to stay. The temptation to do so was growing by the minute. Time was running out and I knew I had to decide. I fought my default for comfort and accepted the transfer.

The rest is history. I thought that I, at least, took a semi-related role as an instructional designer but I had no clue how far away from HR I had really pushed myself until I was sitting across the conference table one day from a senior leader in finance who spoke so fast in finance jargon that I was certain she was speaking a foreign language. In some ways, she was! Immediately, I felt ten times smaller, regretting my decision to take the role. How was I going to support this department when I know nothing about finance, accounting, or revenue-cycle?

I thought I was done with exams after passing the one I needed to be granted an interview and ultimately, the job. The universe thought otherwise. I hate exams but after talking to a mentor, I decided it was time to speed learn what I needed to so that I could support the finance division I was now servicing. So, I dug into my personal savings and took a self-paced course and another exam to become certified in revenue-cycle.

Looking back, it was money well spent because it taught me how connected every department, division, and role was (and should be) in a company. In the end, a company fails if all parts do not work together. I signed up for an instructional design job in the IT department, but I needed to know a lot more than my job and my department. I needed to support an entire finance division in an incredibly intimate way. I also needed to understand insurance and risk management since that was so connected to finance. I even needed to tap into my HR background because of the impacts to the financials.

As luck would have it, this entire experience changed the trajectory of my career but, more notably, it also shifted the perspective by which I would lead HR when I was recruited back into the field. I could now clearly see all the dots as well as how to connect them. I *needed* to leave HR to see this.

I want to be clear: we don't all have to transfer out of our current field to gain this insight. But for me, it was certainly a powerful way to accomplish this. This is not an option for everyone right now. So, what are some other ways to accomplish the same thing?

Other Ways to Get Out of HR

Getting out of HR does not have to be so literal. There are so many ways to do this and gain the benefits of going beyond our comfort zone, what we already know, and our own beliefs and biases. Leaving HR can allow us to expand our horizons, truly understand the business we support, share our world with others, and build trust as well as relationships.

So, how else can we get out of HR? This is, by no means, an exhaustive list but they are great places to start. There is an easy-to-read inforgraphic available using the link in the back of the book.

Initiate and Attend Meetings

Initiating and attending leadership, department, division, and company meetings allows us, as members of HR, to stay in-the-know about the company and the areas that we support. I once had an incredible HR Business Partner on my team who did just this. Her name was Laura and she was a self-motivated, collaborative team member who had a genuine interest in making a positive impact.

When she started her role on my team, it had been decades since she had worked in HR. There were questions from others within the company as to whether she was the right fit for the role and our department. However, I knew, without a doubt, that her time away from HR was going to be invaluable to us. She had spent the last couple of decades dedicated to her kids as a mom and then took on entry and mid-level roles within our operational and IT departments.

I was told I was taking a gamble on, and with, Laura; but, quite frankly, I thought the odds were stacked in our favor. Regardless, the team was ready to provide her all the support and guidance she needed.

However, it quickly became clear that she was not going to need as much guidance and support as some may have thought. The first thing Laura did when she took the job was set up meetings with all our department and division heads, asked them for invites to their leadership and department/division meetings, and requested shadow opportunities (more on this later) with their team members.

See, many people in this situation would have defaulted to learning what they could about HR, *our* department, or the role in which they were hired for, before anything else. Not Laura. She knew she could learn that in time. Plus, she had prior experience, so she was not starting from scratch. What Laura instinctively knew that others may not is that to be successful in any role and department in the company, she had to have strong relationships that were built on trust. She knew that no organization runs successfully in silos. She knew that she had to learn how to connect the dots, for herself and for others. To do this, she had to get out of HR, not stay in it.

The operational leaders and team members, alike, used to tell me how different she was than other HR professionals they had worked with and how her approach was so refreshing. They took notice of the effort she put in to get to know them, their work, and their teams. She was initiating and asking to sit in on meetings and shadowing team members. Her efforts were respected. They appreciated that she didn't just use conventional HR practices and methods like reciting policies to them, trying to force irrelevant precedence to every situation, or only focusing on the HR-aspect of a problem. I couldn't agree more.

Needless to say, she surpassed expectations in no time and I'm proud to share that she now runs a divisional HR Business Partner team at that same organization.

Shadow Other Areas

Similar to attending meetings, shadowing is also a fantastic way to learn about the people, functions, and business lines that we support. Remember, this was one of the first things that Laura did when she started in her role as an HR Business Partner.

While meetings helped Laura learn about the company and the updates from her departments and divisions that she supported, shadowing allowed her to really gain a true and deeper understanding for the important work that was being done every single day by her operational colleagues. More importantly, shadowing helped Laura gain insights into what people loved most about their jobs, their leaders, their teams, their departments, and the company. As well as what created challenges and obstacles for them.

This information was integral to how Laura approached her role as an HR Business Partner. She knew that not every department or team member had the same needs. What she learned through shadowing allowed her to customize HR strategies and initiatives that would better align with the business and the needs of the employees. It also led to meaningful and positive changes to company and department policies as well as to the overall employee experience.

Laura didn't just create credibility for herself; but rather her commitment to her stakeholders helped improve the credibility and reputation of the entire HR department.

Conduct Rounds

There are many roles within HR and not all of them are structured the same. Not every role has distinct stakeholder groups assigned to them. Some HR professionals are a team of one for the entire company and some are part of a bigger team but still responsible for supporting the entire company. Perhaps, some of us are an HR leader who is also responsible for overseeing policies, practices, programs, and services that impact everyone. So, attending every department and division meeting or shadowing every single department may not be a realistic option.

However, conducting rounds can have a similar benefit. Rounding with different departments across the company allows us to build relationships, learn the business, and improve our HR services. A major benefit to rounding is that this can be done over time and on a continuous basis. This is helpful so that it is not too overwhelming in addition to our daily work.

Another benefit of rounding is that it can provide the combined results of attending meetings and shadowing. It allows us to stay updated on the happenings of the company on a more regular basis and gives us a deeper appreciation for the daily operations, challenges, and experiences of our team members and each unique department.

Participate in A Non-HR Project

If we want to dive even deeper, we can participate in, raise our hand for, or say yes to joining a non-HR project. This is a great way to get out of our offices and away from our homebase and really get to know another side of the business.

When I was early in my career, such an opportunity presented itself and, initially, I hesitated. Ultimately, I decided to take a leap of faith and I have no regrets. My organization was certifying several employees from different departments as Lean Six Sigma Green Belts, which is a process improvement certification. I was nominated by my executive leader at the time and my certification projects were in operational departments, not HR. To put it plainly, I was terrified.

I wondered "What if I don't pass the test after they invested in me to get trained?" "What if I just can't grasp the concepts because they were so different from anything I've ever done?" "What if I fail the projects or they don't produce the expected results or improvements?"

Then, I remembered something that my dear uncle, who had a huge influence on my life since the day that I was born, said to me once when I was afraid to do something as a teenager. I heard his voice so clearly, "What is the worst that could realistically happen, what is the best-case scenario, and would the best-case scenario be worth it to you in the end?"

It was his way of guiding me to do it, even if I do it scared. So, I channeled that energy and took on the projects and the certification scared. I learned so much, not just about process improvement but about how other departments work and how everyone's role within the company was so tied together. It taught me that the more we understand each other's roles within the bigger picture, the more empathy we can develop, and the more successful we *will* be because we are able to better collaborate with each other.

Breaking down silos and building relationships outside of our own immediate work functions is so critical in our ability to create success for the company. From there, we are able to grow our own skills, knowledge, and careers.

Participate in Company Events

Cross-functional relationships can also be built and nurtured through participation in company events. This can mean anything from a company volunteer day, to an award celebration, to a company retreat. These events can bring people together outside of work in ways that naturally create positive team building and bonding. Because these events happen outside the normal scope of the workday, it brings a level of familiarity, personality, and individuality to the people on various teams within the company. This only serves to help us forge bonds and build relationships. It is a basis for a strong foundation.

Go on A Site Visit

Sometimes, learning the business means that we will need to look both externally and internally. One way to do this is a site visit to another company, a vendor, or a client. Site visits provide the opportunity to learn from others in the business so that we can bring back ideas and improvements to make within our own company.

I remember taking on the task to lead a new Human Resource Information System HRIS) implementation. I had never used this system before, nor had anyone in our department, or anyone else that I could find in the company. So, I reached out to a competitor to see if they would be willing to host my team, show us how they built their system, and discuss lessons learned and tips.

Some of my team and my peers thought it was silly of me to reach out to a competitor because "Why would a competitor want to share knowledge with us?" That would certainly take away their competitive advantage, right?

To my team's and peers' surprise, I got an immediate "yes" and scheduled a site visit rather quickly. It was an incredible learning experience, and the "competition" was not only gracious in sharing information with us, but they were also generous in their time and went above and beyond to support us throughout our entire implementation; not just during the site visit.

Whenever we ran into a question or issue that our consultants even struggled to figure out, I'd give this other organization a call and get insights on how to resolve our situation or problem. It was a lesson in the abundance mindset. There are plenty of people ready and willing to help even if they were a direct competitor.

When we support each other, we create more opportunities for everyone, not less. We make the industry better, the business world better, and the community better. Not worse.

Now that we have gained some valuable insights about the impact of an external site visit, it is also important to call out the power of internal site visits. That is, if our company has multiple sites, visiting the different sites *within* our company can help us understand our internal customers better.

In HR, it is ever more significant to have a strong grasp of our internal stakeholders and what the employee experience really feels like at each location, in each department, and for each individual. To understand how to do this and the benefits it yields, I'll point us back to Laura and her ability to do this by visiting the different departments. The benefits are the same.

Attend A Variety of Events

Continuing the theme of learning from external parties, another way to do this is attending a variety of events. This could be a conference, a think tank, a networking event, an industry meeting, or a professional development activity.

I asked Paul LaLonde, also known as the HR Philosopher, what he felt really helped him become the respected and successful HR leader that he is today. He shared an experience early on in his career where he did not network as much and reach out to others. At that time. it was not in his comfort zone to network; but once he *did* decide to step out of his comfort zone, things really opened up for him. He started getting involved with his fellow peers in the HR space and eventually attended big and small conferences that introduced him to even more critical relationships that would help him as he progressed in his career.

Paul does not just attend HR conferences, though. He attends conferences in the nonprofit sector and even industry-specific events. When he worked with Meals on Wheels, he attended their conferences. When he worked in transit, he attended transit-specific events.

Paul recounted numerous times when he called up someone within his network to ask them for feedback on a topic he was not familiar with or to connect them with someone he knew would be a great addition to *their* network. He is the definition of "networking and industry events done right" because he understands the professional, personal, *and* social benefits.[1]

Take A Class

To take things even further, Paul invested in getting certifications beyond HR such as receiving his Certified Community Action Professional (CCAP) designation. Whether it comes with formal credentials or not, investing in learning about other functions, industries, or professions can help us better relate to people and gain credibility faster because we can speak their language.

Personally, I've taken courses or gained certifications in business, revenue cycle, process improvement, healthcare operations, finance and accounting, digital marketing, and global studies, to name a few. All of these have helped me become a more rounded HR leader and jump into operational conversations and strategy discussions that may not be directly related to

---

1. Paul LaLonde [Interview]. 24 March 2024

HR. They have also allowed me to connect with people faster so that relationship building beyond just work was easier.

Casual Meetups

Who said getting out of HR wasn't fun? Getting out of HR does not always have to be formal. It can also be a casual meeting, or meetup. Maybe it's an ad-hoc catch-up meeting, maybe it's lunch, or maybe it's another outing that we know the person we're meeting with enjoys (coffee, happy hour, trivia, etc.). This allows us to not only learn from others in regard to their work, but *also* about them as humans. Personalization in relationship building is not just helpful, it's key. Knowing people holistically allows us to better work together and connect with them on a deeper level.

When I entered the startup space, I knew I had to get up-to-speed fast. So, I started scheduling casual catch-ups with my team members and my peers, and even some employees from different departments. Sure, we would talk about *some* business, but the point of these catch/meet-ups was just to get to know and connect with team members on a personal level.

There are so many ways to do this, but as HR professionals, there can be true joy in leaving our departments, our offices, and our companies to make our HR function, our companies, and ourselves even better. We can never truly know it all, so learning from others helps us think in a more innovative way. Having a strong network allows us to "phone a friend" when we need some help, someone to bounce ideas around, or encouragement.

Inviting Others In

Point taken, right? Getting out of HR is critical for building relationships, learning the business, and improving HR strategy. There is also a bonus method that I would be remiss not to mention. That is: invite others in.

Guess what? We can be party crashers and party throwers at the same time. Why not hold an HR Open House or invite others to HR for an event like a benefits fair, a lunch and learn, HR Appreciation Day, or HR Professionals Day? Even better, invite others to be involved in HR projects and initiatives. Too scary? Do it scared. Do it anyway.

Taking opportunities to invite and bring people into our space, our day, our department, our roles, and our profession allows them to feel included in HR. It makes HR way less scary and way more fun, interesting, meaningful, and trustworthy.

The next time there is an initiative to push out – benefits enrollment, employee experience survey, or a new policy – why not invite others *in* to learn about it instead of just simply sending *out* an email announcement? We can take these opportunities to not just share about what we are doing, but also build relationships and show that HR knows how to have some fun.

Learning the business helps us align our strategy, initiatives, and programs in a way that helps everyone succeed. It improves the entire team member experience when we break down the silos and truly find ways to work better *together*. It can also be super exciting, interesting, and humbling to learn and grow *beyond* HR. There are so many fascinating people yet to learn from and to meet. Even beyond the bounds and scope of HR.

Let's love our people and *let* them love us back. Whether it is physically and/or virtually leaving HR or inviting others into HR, the ability to share space with others and learn from them is a gift. The joy of HR does not just lie within the walls of HR. Let's get out of HR to spread more joy and, trust me, we will receive more joy in return.

Chapter 2

The Joy of Solving Real Problems

Get Out of Our Heads

IT WAS PROBABLY the tenth meeting that I sat in. I was listening to how one of our departments was losing revenue and no one could figure out why. Lots of hypotheses were discussed. Lots of trial and error. No resolution.

I could tell it was getting a bit tense for everyone, people were clearly frustrated, and I had a hunch that maybe my team could help. So, I volunteered my team to do just that: help. We received some odd stares since we're "just HR." How could *we* figure something out that the "business people" hadn't even figured out yet?

I sat patiently and waited until the desperation set in. Reluctantly, an agreement was made for us, "just HR," to see what we could do to help. So, we got to work. Remember that Lean Six Sigma Green Belt certification I fearfully obtained? Well, it ended up being exactly what we needed.

My team and I did a root cause analysis. We interviewed the team members, the leaders, and impacted stakeholders. We also conducted observations and investigated the business and financial data that was available. What we learned was that, within this department, 90-day turnover was incredibly high and only trending higher each month. This caused a huge disruption to the daily operations and was even starting to impact the ability to open some locations of the business every day. This was negatively affecting both the employee and customer experience. Thus, customer turnover was also rapidly increasing, and thus revenue was being negatively impacted.

So we asked, "What has caused the high 90-day turnover?" We were able to break it down to two things.

- The first was the lack of ***onboarding***. Team members felt like they were thrown into a job they did not sign up for and one that they did not feel prepared to perform appropriately. They received a "buddy" on day one to shadow and then, on day two, they were on their own. By then, they felt abandoned or left to drown alone if they had questions or did not know how to do something.

- The second issue was ***scheduling***. The team was asked to travel to multiple sites but they were not told that this would be an expected part of their job/role during the interview or offer. Some members of the team were traveling to sites an hour – or more – from home. Related to onboarding, they were also expected to do things differently at each location but were not trained on how to do this. People who were hired for certain hours were not working those hours. People who had previously confirmed their regular days off were no longer receiving those days off. All the scheduling went through one person, so the team was not even allowed to find coverage for themselves. If someone called off sick, the whole schedule would be chaotic because of how people were moved around.

We presented our findings but there was a lot of skepticism. How could this all be because of something so simple...so HR? There must be something else.

Except there wasn't. So, we implemented an action plan to build and maintain a significantly improved onboarding and scheduling process. It took several months to see the impact but once we were able to measure it, we saw the 90-day turnover decrease. At the same time, we watched employee experience scores and customer experience scores increase. Customer turnover decreased, and revenue increased again.

That's right. Revenue started increasing again! No more productivity was lost with new hires. No more time wasted by leaders constantly interviewing for new candidates. No more frustration over scheduling issues. No more extra workload falling to employees who stay because of being short-staffed. No more closing locations because that location was not well-staffed. No more losing customers.

We could have put our heads down and focused on transactional HR tasks but there is a special trust built when we, in HR, can help solve *real* business problems. When others start to see the results of that, solutions to *real* business problems, credibility increases for our teams as well as for our profession.

As wonderful as that story was, we do not always have to solve problems in such dramatic ways. It can be done by simply being more thoughtful and intentional in how we lead our HR functions.

It took me a long time to really understand who I was and who I wanted to be as an HR leader and settle into my own approach. Once I did, magic happened, or something like that. What I realized is that society and the industry has drilled into us this core philosophy that we must follow "best practices." What does that even mean?

We've been trained to simply look to see what most other people have done and follow their lead. But where has that actually led us? Certainly, to some more innovative HR practices, but also to some questionable trends. Think performative DEI initiatives, antiquated leave of absence policies, arbitrary recruitment requirements, and unproductive performance management processes.

When it finally hit me that all I was doing was reinforcing what the majority of others have done (and what many were still doing at the time), I felt disappointed and cynical about our profession. I was confused about my own place in it, and frustrated about how to move forward for my company, my team, and myself.

This led me down the path of taking a lot more risks, and purposeful ones, at that. I started piloting and pushing out more progressive, productive, and prolific initiatives. As expected though, this was received by others with utter shock, major push back, and extreme doubt like I have never experienced before. However, it began to shape my approach to HR, change management, and frankly, life. I started leading with greater intention, rather than following the status quo.

So, how do we lead HR with greater intention and purpose so we can solve real problems, rather than just ones that we made up or someone made up for us?

While it is not an exhaustive list, there are four main beliefs that I think can help HR professionals and leaders truly transform HR into one of the most, if not *the* most, valued department in a company.

    1. Make a point to understand the business.

    2. Make a point to understand HR.

    3. Make a point to engage in purposeful action.

4. Make a point to engage genuinely with people.

These beliefs allow us to shift our mindsets and approaches in a way that gives us the freedom to focus on solving real problems, rather than making assumptions and spending our time on things that do not make a difference in the end. They're simple in theory, but intricate in practice.

Make A Point to Understand the Business

I sound like a broken record with this one, but it is so important if we want to make a difference in our places of work. Chapter 1 talks about how to do this but the first step is actually a mindset shift.

We, as HR professionals, need to truly believe that we are a strategic and necessary part of the business. We need to know that we have a *direct* impact on that business, and that our value is no different than operations, marketing, finance, IT, or any other function. In business, it doesn't take two to tango; it actually takes a whole orchestra of people to tango!

It is only until we believe this in the deepest part of our hearts and minds that we can really start to learn and understand the business. Then, we must seriously embed ourselves within that business to learn the ins and outs of our business strategy, goals, operations, key performance indicators (KPIs), and core needs. This in-depth information allows us to align HR to the business in a much more impactful manner.

In addition, we must also work to understand the desires, perspectives, stories, and experiences of our people at all levels of the organization because *this* is paramount to the culture and success of the business.

Make A Point to Understand HR

So, we get the business. Now, do we *get* HR? I know, that seems like a silly question to ask. Of course we get HR! We *are* HR! That's not what I mean, though.

We must go beyond a basic, or even a deep, understanding of HR functions. We must go beyond understanding policies, processes, and programs.

- How can HR help the business, as a whole, be more successful?

- How can HR better impact the bottom line?

- How can HR help solve a major business problem successfully?

- How can HR help lead a big change in the business in a people-centric way?

- How can HR support revenue generation, or cost-savings, without negatively impacting culture and productivity?

- How can we help keep people supported, and also motivated, in tough times?

These are the more complex questions we must start asking, and answering, if we want to really understand HR, its role, and its impact in the company. Adding to the worthy challenge is that we must *understand* these questions as it relates to every part of the employee lifecycle from candidate attraction and employer branding all the way to post-employment and alumni relations.

Make a Point to Engage in Purposeful Action

Once we have a strong grasp of the business and how HR can make purposeful and meaningful impacts on that business, we can finally take action.

To take purposeful action, we must first be able to think purposefully. As HR professionals, it can sometimes feel like we are stuck between the wishes, perspectives, and expectations of our employees and those of senior leadership. These elements between employees and senior leadership are often dichotomous and quite polarizing.

I'll never forget presenting low employee experience scores to an executive team. I had barely started the presentation. I think I was on slide three or four when I was rudely interrupted. The team was sidetracked and distracted about why the scores were so low. It was concluded that there was nothing we could do about the scores that year because the low scores were, in whole, due to employees' dissatisfaction with their pay being lower than expected; and, of course, we did not have the budget to increase pay.

This was not a totally unfair hypothesis as we had heard complaints about low pay, and we knew an overhaul of the compensation program was necessary. My team and I actually had a similar hypothesis when we first saw the survey results. However, I had learned intentional leadership by this point and wanted to be more accurate in our analysis. So, I knew we all needed to get out of our own heads, and out of our own way. I urged the team to hold their reasonable hypothesis and allow my team to continue with a root cause analysis beyond the survey results.

We held focus groups at all levels within the company, we participated in department meetings and embedded ourselves into the business, and we implemented pulse surveys to ask more specific questions and get a more frequent measure of employee experience.

Sure enough, we learned that the low employee experience scores were not directly due to low pay.

It was certainly an indirect factor, but team members shared that they would not leave *just* because of low pay. They also shared that the low scores and high turnover were really happening because of unbearable staffing issues and burnout.

Guess what? That *is* something we could address and had control over; and, honestly, it was not going to cost us much at all. So, how did we solve the problem?

The obvious solution might have been to increase headcount; that is, add staff members. Some people probably would even call that best practice, but if it was that simple, the problem would have already been solved. An important point to remember is that we had no money to increase headcount.

Plus, during our research, we found that the root cause was not just the number of people working. We also heard about poor leadership, time off policies and how they were being enforced, lack of training, the impacts that the COVID-19 pandemic had on the demands of the job, and much, much more.

We tackled the root causes. We:

- quickly built, launched, and measured an interactive customized leadership development program

- revamped our time off policy and communicated it to team members repeatedly via multiple channels

- implemented a confidential grievance and compliance process

- rebuilt the onboarding process and worked with functional leaders to create role-based training

- and restructured the staffing model to accommodate the needs of our team members without increasing headcount

We saw an exponential increase in employee experience scores in the pulse surveys as well as with the more in-depth annual survey. The more exciting trend, though, was the positive and unexpected (well, not to us in HR but to some in the business) impact to business results like productivity, revenue, and even budget.

Make A Point to Engage Genuinely with People

None of these results would have been possible, however, without people, relationships, and trust – all of which are intimately connected. To be able to execute people-solutions for business problems successfully, people across the company needed to believe in us; in our HR team.

The CEO and executive team senior leadership) had to trust us enough to back our ideas and, ultimately, our proposals for solutioning. The middle leadership needed to believe that we would genuinely help them, rather than hinder or micromanage them, to allow us into their meetings and be embedded into their operations. The team members had to have enough confidence in us to be honest in the focus groups and in their feedback about the issues they were experiencing.

But, why? Why *would* they trust us? Well, that trust didn't happen overnight. In fact, it was an ongoing process and because we, as an HR team, wholeheartedly believed that it was a continuous process, team members and leadership alike knew we were serious and authentic in our relationship-building. Between my team and me, we knew the names and stories of every single employee. We wanted them to know that we saw them as whole humans, not just workers in a chair or numbers on a roster.

Because we absolutely and intentionally cared about and for our team members and the company, we were able to solve a very real business problem that was affecting business outcomes.

Intentional thinking and acting allowed us to do things differently, to bring about positive changes, and to address the root causes of issues rather than just checking a box. We were able to speak up, step up, and stand up for what was and is right rather than worrying about making everyone happy (which is an unrealistic goal that does not usually solve the real problem).

To solve real problems, we must understand the problems – what they are, the root causes, and people's perspectives and feelings about the problems. To understand the problems, we must get out of our own heads and go where the problems exist. To get out of our own heads, we must learn the business, engage in purposeful action, and engage genuinely with our people.

Chapter 3

The Joy
of Communicating
Effectively

Get Out of Our Assumptions

"You'll probably hear about him at some
point in your first few months here. He's
a pain in everyone's side and cannot be
reasoned with. Don't even try. If he gives
you any trouble, just escalate it. Everyone
knows he's impossible to work with and

he's unwilling to do anything we tell him to do to solve his problems. This has been going on for years. Actually longer. It's been going on since he started here. No one likes working with him. Just want to warn you."

THIS IS THE introduction I received for a leader of a prominent division within a company I worked for. This was not just my newly inherited team's account of this person, but my boss's account as well. Little did they know, their description of this leader didn't make me dread meeting him for the first time. If anything, it made me very much look forward to my first encounter.

I proactively reached out for a meet-and-greet. Honestly, it was rather pleasant. I was asked about the meet-and-greet by the team and was told that his pleasant demeanor was fake and that they had felt the same way the first time they met him. That is, until there was an issue to deal with. So, I waited. I waited until that day came.

"Ping!"

A new email had entered my inbox.

Alas, the day had come. One of my team members had copied nearly my entire chain of command on an email full of clear frustration. They really had it with this leader and refused to work with him again.

I've worked for years on my impatience and my need to respond to everything immediately, so I wasn't about to waste all those years of lessons learned. Instead, I read the email once; and, then, I read it again. Afterwards, I sat there reflecting on the situation, thinking about my team member's reaction, and trying to remove any bias from my analysis.

Before I could finish my thought process, I heard another," Ping!"

It was my boss. They had already replied. They shared and held the same frustration as my team member and responded with something along the lines of, "I'll handle it. I have a meeting with the CEO this afternoon, and will escalate."

This complicated my reflection, my thoughts, my analysis. How do I handle this one? Everyone's already getting involved before I even had the chance to respond or step in.

I started writing down my assumptions and what I believed were the assumptions of my peers. That made me realize I did not have enough information to even begin to solve the problem. There were still so many questions left unanswered.

So, I video chatted with my boss (I know, I leveled up my technology with this job). I asked if they would be agreeable to me taking this situation on and handling it. They chuckled and shockingly exclaimed, "Really?"

I fired back, "Yes, I feel like that would be the appropriate next step."

I was met with another chuckle before they said, "Well, heck, if you want to take this on, go for it! Makes my day if I don't have to deal with him!"

Great! I called up this infamous leader, caught up with him, and explained why I was calling. I shared the report I was provided in regards to a situation in his division. I was met with an eye roll but withheld judgment or a reactive response.

I asked him to share his perspective. More importantly, I asked him how his team was doing, given the situation. He was surprised and shared that no one has ever cared enough to ask that question.

He shared a different perspective. I asked a series of questions. He validated some of what was in the report and shed some light on some things that were missing or inaccurate. He offered up his team for further conversations to ensure we got to an appropriate resolution.

Ultimately, we landed on a solution, together, that worked for all parties. Weeks after the solution had already been put in place, I was asked how things were going with that leader and the problems in his department. Everyone seemed to be in complete disbelief that the issue had already been resolved without incident.

The joke apparently became that this leader was "my new best friend" because I was actually able to work with him successfully when no one else ever had before.

What I learned, though, is that the leader did not feel heard or communicated with well in the past. He felt talked to or at (not with), demeaned, and reprimanded every time something happened in his division. In fact, he started feeling like HR was purposely looking for things to get him in trouble, rather than being there to help.

He dreaded an email, video call, phone call, text, or chat message from our department. That "Ping!" triggered fear and anxiety within him. He said if he saw or heard that "Ping!," it would ruin his day before he even heard or read the message. He said he knew it meant that he was about to be scolded and wouldn't be able to share his or his team's perspective because it would be immediately shut down.

It was a reminder that communication is not one-way, and that listening is an extraordinarily critical part of effective communication. It was a lesson that I, too, had learned the hard way through mistakes made in the past.

Communication can be messy and complicated sometimes, too. As in my above example, I couldn't just take some sequential steps and be done. It was communicated to me verbally about this leader, then via email about an issue with the leader, then with my boss about who would handle the situation, then with the leader about the situation, and so on.

The key to successful communication, though, is being able to step out of and away from our assumptions. Humans are biased, complex, and imperfect. We sometimes say things that we do not mean or hear something that the person communicating did not mean. That is when assumptions come into play.

A process to keep us all accountable is one I like to call AAC. Here is what it means and what it looks like in practice.

When communicating to others, we ACKNOWLEDGE our assumptions, ASK for feedback and perspectives, and COMMIT to continuing honest, clear, and respectful communication.

Similarly, when receiving communication from others, we ACKNOWLEDGE our assumptions, ASK for clarification, and COMMIT to continuing honest, clear, and respectful communication.

It may seem simple, but these communication tactics are not used nearly enough. I really, fully developed this when I was working for a company that was so appalled by a specific score on their employee experience results, the pay and benefits score. It was the lowest score year after year ever since we had started the survey process.

We reached out to the third-party survey company to inquire about how they have seen other companies improve this score. The survey company said that it was very common for this to be the lowest score and that we were in line with the benchmark. However, we were not satisfied. I was not satisfied. My boss was not satisfied. My executive team was not satisfied.

If the survey company can't tell us, we thought, "Well, let's ask the people who filled out the survey."

In our communication, we shared that this score was troubling to us and that we had made improvements to our pay and benefits over the years without improvement in the score. We acknowledged our assumption that the score was low simply because people *felt* they were not paid well or did not *think* we had good benefits. However, improvements to those things did not lead to improvement in the score. Thus, we believed there was more to the score and to the experience our employees were having with our pay and benefits. This was us ACKNOWLEDGING our assumptions.

We, then, asked two questions. The first was which benefits employees were aware of that we offered. The second asked what about our pay program was not satisfactory, with a list of options including "other." This was us ASKING for feedback and perspective.

We were amazed at the results! Particularly, the fact that most employees had no clue about many of our benefits and that they were less disappointed about their actual pay as they were about *how* pay was determined. They felt that everyone was given a salary but had no idea what their salary range or grade was or how those were determined or what benchmark criteria or sources were used to determine pay. Transparency is key here.

We were solving the wrong problems, all because of a lack of communication. We couldn't just stop at a single survey and make assumptions.

So, we started a campaign to ensure that benefits were repeatedly communicated throughout the year and that employees were receiving information that was most relevant to them. We also worked towards a pay transparency program and communicated with our team members along the way. This was us

COMMITTING to continuing honest, clear, and respectful communication.

It worked! The very next year, we saw the pay and benefits score on the survey increase by what the survey company said was an "unheard of" amount.

Another relevant example is how companies are communicating, or not communicating, about their return-to-work policies and expectations after the COVID-19 pandemic. Cat Colella-Graham is a communication expert who has advised, coached, and led many teams through these changes. What she realized as a common root cause of the problem is that employees do not understand *why* they are being forced back to an office. Many companies have simply required employees to return to an on-site office with the threat that if they do not, they will no longer be employed. No explanation. No communication.

The assumption that employees should have just *known* that things would go back to how they were prior to COVID is quite problematic. If we hadn't changed our policies, or our mindsets from a global pandemic, perhaps, we hadn't learned much from it after all. We forced our team members to completely change their lives overnight to adjust to companies' needs when COVID hit. So, many companies assumed that those same team members would, again, readjust immediately to *their* desire to go back to pre-COVID times.

While many feel they can do their jobs remotely forever, there can be some benefits to onsite work for some teams, companies, or industries. Cat has supported companies to better communicate as they bring people back to more in-person collaborations while keeping attrition low and maintaining a positive employee experience. She shared some key takeaways including:

- Ensuring that leaders, managers, and employees all receive the same message,

- Holding info sessions to help employees understand why the company is asking them to return two days per week to the office, and

- Creating moments that matter for employees while they are onsite, rather than simply requiring them to come in and take virtual meetings.

Creating and communicating the moments that matter may be one of the most critical points as other companies look to improve their employee experience in a new hybrid work environment. Cat shared some ways that she helped companies do just this.

First, it is important for companies and company leaders to understand their objective – what they are *actually* trying to achieve by asking employees to come back to the office or moving towards a hybrid model. It is even more important that these leaders listen to their employees to understand the barriers to success and share how the company will address, solve, or break down those barriers to support employees. For example, if commuting or parking is the issue, then companies need to consider ways to solve that – carpooling programs, public transportation support, or financial support and reimbursements for transit cards.

Cat has worked with HR and People departments to support such a change by ensuring that they are considering, addressing, and communicating the benefits, challenges, reasons, and resources related to the change. [1]

We often think that a lack of communication is due to us not communicating enough, not listening enough, not speaking up enough, or not saying something clearly enough. All of this certainly plays a critical part in communication, but the root cause of many communication issues is our assumptions.

Just think about how many times we've heard any, if not all, of the following thoughts, or assumptions:

- That employees should know when they are not doing a good job.

- My boss can't possibly think they are a good leader.

---

1. Cat Colella-Graham [Interview]. 9 January 2024

- How do they not know that already?!

- What were they thinking?!

- Are they out of their mind?!

These are all thoughts that stem from assumptions about people.

- It's likely employees may not know they're not doing a good job if we have not told them that.

- It's likely our boss *does* think they are a good leader if we have not shared that we are experiencing them differently.

- It's possible that something that seems simple to *us* can seem complicated to *someone else*.

- It's possible that something that seems obvious to us is not obvious to others because they, simply, do not have the same information, perspective, or experience as we do.

- It's okay that others have a different opinion or perspective than us and can still be totally coherent and not "out of their minds."

A people leader I admire, Sarika Lamont, recalls a peer of hers on the executive team questioning why people were shocked and upset when they conducted a layoff. Didn't they know that the business was suffering? Don't they know what is going on in the economy?

She pushed back, and she pushed back hard. She reminded them of how there had not been any communication about the business, the company's financials, or the economy that was coming from the leadership team. If they wanted people to know something, it needed to be communicated – not just told, but *actually* communicated. Actual communication means sharing information, seeking feedback, listening to how it impacts people, making changes, and then recommunicating.

So, she helped her executive team implement communication programs and practices that were more transparent, frequent, and meaningful. Sure enough, there was eventually another layoff, but it was received much better than the first. People saw it coming, they felt involved, and they felt supported.

No one made assumptions about how the employees should have felt or what they should have known. [2]

Assumptions keep us from communicating well. To communicate effectively, we must get out of our assumptions. And, trust me, it is pure joy to do so!

---

2. Sarika Lamont [Interview]. 7 February 2024

Chapter 4

The Joy of Doing the Right Thing

Get Out of Our Comfort Zones

"All I did was repeat what she already told you."

THESE WORDS HIT me right in the heart. They were said, in addition to several other beautiful things, by my direct superior (an executive leader) after one of his peers berated me in front of an entire room of our team members. On top of that, these team members were at all levels of the organization, and he used words I won't share here.

I had respectfully shared with the executive that his desire to fire people for sharing their salary with each other would not only be potentially unlawful but that it was not the appropriate mindset and approach to improve the employee experience. His division had astonishingly low survey scores and we were meeting about compensation review as one of the strategies.

After he yelled at me for "not knowing what I was talking about" and screaming, to make sure I heard him that "he can absolutely fire people for whatever reason he wanted," my boss intervened and repeated almost verbatim what I had already explained to him.

While he deemed me incompetent for the exact same statement, he thanked my boss for sharing the information and apologized to my boss for not knowing the implications. To my pleasant surprise, this annoyed my boss who jumped to my defense and passionately, but civilly, told his peer (in front of the entire group) that he was out of line for questioning my intelligence, dismissing me, raising his voice at me, and then turning around responding positively to *him* for saying the same exact thing as I already had.

My boss had sent a message by speaking up. Not just to one person but to many. My boss was the final step of our grievance process, appeal process, and termination review process. Everyone knew that. This meant that the person ultimately responsible for such decisions would not tolerate sexism, racism, or ageism.

Was this outside of my boss's comfort zone? I'm not entirely sure, but he was willing to do something uncomfortable in order to create a powerful and positive change. He took a risk. This was someone he had to continue working with on a day-to-day basis. The person in question was his direct peer and a senior executive at the same exact level. To put it frankly: he was someone with power in the company.

My boss didn't care though. He only cared about doing the right thing at that moment.

It wasn't exactly an easy thing for him to do but doing the right thing is not always easy. If it was, trust me, more people would choose to do what is right.

It's no secret that workplaces still have a long way to go when it comes to ethical and inclusive leadership. Unfortunately, there is no secret that will solve this overnight, either. It is an ongoing process of improvement that we must commit to in order for us to even start seeing progress.

The key is to *start*. When people ask me how to start, my response is usually, "Speak up, stand up, and step up. Sounds simple but it's not. It takes courage. Sometimes, it even takes willpower, resilience, and a lot of risk. Yet, it is necessary, and it is one way to *start*."

Speak Up

Speaking up is what my boss did that day when he heard and saw someone who was demeaning and belittling. He used his voice and power to put a stop to a peer's inappropriate behavior...behavior that was offensive to a room full of people involved and was making them incredibly uncomfortable.

Our voices may not seem like much when we're not in a position of power; but, in fact, our voices hold an unbelievable amount of power. This is true regardless of our position and status.

I remember being in a room as a new employee. I had no credibility or goodwill built up yet. My team shared with me something that they had been instructed – actually, it was demanded of them – to do. It was something that they did not feel was morally appropriate. They said that they fought as hard as they could but were told that it was not up to them, and they needed to do as they were told. In a meeting on the topic, I spoke up first and made as strong of a business case as I could to not move forward with the request.

Maybe being new made them go easy on me, or maybe they heard something from me that struck a chord and elicited a change of heart, or maybe it was all luck. Either way, I, nor my team, thought my voice would do much that day. I decided to try using it anyway and it worked. It prevented a disaster for our employees, our team, and the company.

We all have something important to say and while it may not be heard one hundred percent of the time, our voices matter, and our voices could mean everything to someone.

Stand Up

Our voices could even mean that we are standing up for something. There are so many ways to stand up and do the right thing. It might mean anything from owning up to a mistake, to coaching up, or maybe even influencing our superiors to doing something when we see it needs to be done rather than turning away.

Standing up means that if we see something wrong, we do something about it. When we hear something wrong, we say something about it. It is about the will to act when something is not right.

An exceptional HR leader shared a story that highlights the challenges and triumphs in her career.

She recounted a time when her company acquired another just before the pandemic, only to face severe business losses due to COVID-19. Ultimately, the business had to be shut down, and the employees were let go.

During this tumultuous period, her executive counterpart was giving employees false hope that the business would not be sold, urging them to stay motivated and continue their efforts. This misleading communication persisted even up until weeks before the official announcement of the layoffs, despite her efforts to encourage honesty.

This HR leader not only advocated for better communication but also went above and beyond to support the affected employees. She secured strong severance and benefits packages and met personally with the employees to offer support, despite her counterpart's insistence that a simple letter would suffice.

The situation created a rift among the leadership team. Determined to mend this divide, she planned to invest in leadership development to rebuild the team's cohesion. Despite pressure during budget season to cut these funds, she steadfastly refused, presenting a compelling business case. Her persistence paid off, allowing her to maintain the funds and support the leadership team's transformation into a highly functional group.

Step Up

Similarly, stepping up is also about acting when needed, but at an even greater level. It means raising our hand, taking a risk, really stepping out of our comfort zone, or going it alone if no one else is willing to go with us.

You heard about Sarika in the previous chapter. Her journey is so inspiring, and her story is so powerful so I'd like to share another one from her.

Sarika, an HR leader, found herself in a position at a homogenous company having to continuously stand up and speak up for women and employees of color as it related to culture, policies, practices, inclusion and belonging efforts, and business decisions. She pushed for what was right even in an environment that, likely, would not support her.

Sure enough, she was eventually pushed out of that company where she was hired to create positive changes and challenge the status quo. Which is exactly what she had done. In HR, we often find ourselves pushed up with our backs against a wall because we are responsible for, and asked to, execute ethical operations, behaviors, and cultures. Yet, we are not provided the support, resources, or peer accountability to accomplish these responsibilities.

When I asked Sarika if she would change anything, she said no. She knew she did the right thing and speaking up for people who did not always have a seat at the decision-making table was something she saw as her personal responsibility. However, this situation was not over without leaving a lasting impact on Sarika.

Sarika *was* HR, so she didn't have another HR department to reach out to for help. We often forget that there is no one for HR to turn to when they need the same support. When employees, leaders, or even executives, deal with problems, issues, and trauma, they often look to HR to help them. But, what if the person experiencing those problems, issues, and trauma *is* HR? Who do *they* turn to? Who is there to *speak up* for them, *stand up* for them, and *step up* for them?[1]

Ultimately, the idea behind "speak up," "stand up," and "step up," is that no matter who we are, we have a voice. Not only do we have some power to do the right thing, to uphold ethics, and to ensure the safety and belonging of others, it is our responsibility to do what is right. So, if we have privilege, we should use it for good. If we have power, we should use it for good. If we have status, we should use it for good. If we have a voice, we should use it for good. If we have the ability to act, we should use it for good.

To do the right thing, we must be willing to *step up*, *stand up*, and *speak up*. To step up, stand up, and speak up, we sometimes have to stand alone. To stand alone, we often have to be willing to get out of our comfort zones.

Chapter 5

The Joy of Impacting Culture

Get Out of the Way and Get Intentional

EVERYTHING MUST GO through HR. This was the mindset at a company I worked at, and it was not going well. The HR team wanted to be the final say for all decisions and be involved in *every* decision for *every* leader regarding *every* employee. Yet, they complained that they were understaffed and that the operational leaders had no idea what they were doing.

Of course, they didn't. Why would they? We didn't empower them to make decisions on their own or guide them on how to handle employee situations. We didn't give them any tools, except "Call us and let us handle it." Definitely not very empowering, right?

I, too, operated under this mindset for quite some time. The employee experience, including the leadership experience, with HR was not a positive one. I just assumed that the complaints I was hearing from my team were true. It was a "them" problem, not an "us" problem.

Then, I was given the opportunity to lead the function, make necessary changes, and implement new ways of doing things to try and improve the experience with our department. This forced me to do some real, intentional reflection on the current state and the desired outcome; which, in turn, made me realize that our mindset was a huge part of the problem.

My Lean Six Sigma training came in handy again! I did a root cause analysis and learned that our assumptions had been wrong. People did feel the "us" versus "them" mentality and it was not a positive feeling. They felt like HR was only there to find problems, get people in trouble, and fire people.

We didn't just need an operational overhaul, we needed to do some serious service recovery with our stakeholders. We were expecting people to trust us with no credibility, no goodwill, no accountability, and no reciprocation of trust.

We moved away from HR doing everything for people. We worked towards a culture of trust, collaboration, and accountability. It took a lot of very intentional, and sometimes scary, decisions.

We revamped an HR Business Partner team that was solely focused on employee relations issues to one that was focused on true partnership. In other words, we moved from a reactive approach to a proactive one. We moved the team closer to where most of our team members were located, and the hallways became our offices. We operated under the belief that we can't build strong relationships by sitting in our offices all day.

We embedded ourselves into the business. We participated in business meetings, leadership meetings, department meetings, and operational meetings. We got to know:

- people,

- their families,

- their preferences,

- their frustrations,

- what lights them up,

- how they liked to work,

- what they celebrated and how,

- what annoyed them,

- and their ideas for change and improvement.

In other words, we built real relationships. We shadowed and learned about their day-to-day, their lingo, and their micro-cultures within their teams or departments.

We also built an organizational development function that supported the company and the HR business partners by cultivating a culture change. This team also started investing time and energy into developing leaders to be more independent and feel confident in making employee-related decisions on their own. Not the previous "Call us and let us handle it" approach. Our leaders began building muscles for crucial conversations, attracting and retaining top talent, and bringing out the best in their teams.

As these shifts took hold, we began to see better and quicker decisions being made by our leaders who were closer to the everyday work and their people. The complaints about HR dwindled. Overtime, HR actually started proactively being invited to decision and strategy tables proactively. This shift truly happened because we intentionally built a culture of autonomy. To do that successfully, we needed to first build mutual trust and relationships across the company, as well as between HR and the rest of the company.

I shifted my mindset to understand that every behavior, feeling, opinion, or challenge has a reason. To find that reason and truly address and resolve it, we must be able to connect with people.

Our company, at the time, did not have a true business partner function or an organizational development team. Depending on the root cause of the issues we are trying to address within our HR departments, our solutions may look different from company to company but it all comes down to intentionality. Intentional leadership is critical for HR professionals, regardless of whether you consider yourself a formal leader with a title, or not.

Intentional leadership is leading *on* purpose and *with* purpose. It means exemplifying behaviors and making decisions that will create positive impacts for the people and initiatives that we have the privilege of leading. Frankly, I call it "give-a-shit" leadership because if we *actually* care, we can make a difference.

We don't live in a homogenous world, so there is no single "best practice" that will lead us to success. We must think about people's differences and how each company is also unique. One size does not fit all, and fair is not always equal. We need to customize our styles, approaches, and solutions to fit different needs. This seemingly impossible task is made more possible with intention.

My Intentional Leadership Framework, or concept, is a great place to start in becoming a more intentional leader, or HR department. Because, let's be honest, everyone in HR needs to have strong leadership skills. This is, by no means, an exhaustive list of things you must do to be successful, but rather, a guide to support your thinking. The below diagram is available in a printable version at the link in the back of the book.

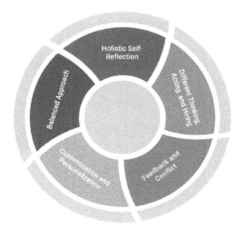

Holistic Self-Reflection

So, where do we begin? It all starts with holistic self-reflection. We hear and talk about self-reflection a lot, but most of us do not actually practice it holistically. True self-reflection is what leads us to true self-awareness, which is a key skill missing not just at work, but in our society as well.

We must go beyond just thinking about what lights us up, what type of work would be most meaningful for us, and what our greatest strengths and values might be. Let me be clear, all those things are critically important, but holistic self-reflection goes deeper. It means that we're engaging in:

- continuous reflection and evaluation of our personal mission,

- default reactions and preferences,

- biases,

- mistakes,

- missteps,

- opportunities,

- annoyances,

- frustrations,

- comfort zones,

- and our *discomfort* zones.

Only then, can we reach a level of real self-awareness that will allow us to lead much more intentionally. It puts everything we do into perspective and allows us to effectively reach the people we lead.

Different Thinking, Acting, and Hiring

Next, we must think, act, and hire differently. We tend to jump to best practices when we enter the "uncomfortable zone," a situation where we do not know what to do. We think, "Well, certainly someone else has done this before!"

This is not actually a bad thing to do, per se. However, intentional leaders and HR professionals go beyond this. We ask what has *not* been thought of yet? We evaluate and assess current situations, processes, initiatives, people, and solutions. We then consider if and how these can be better. We ask, "What is the *right* way to think about this?" instead of simply asking, "What is the way *others* think about this?"

But, we can't think without acting, right? So, it's even more important to *act* differently. What has not been *done* yet?

Intentional HR is about breaking the mold, going against the grain, pushing to do things better and in new ways, fighting for positive changes, and going back to basics when everyone else is chasing the "shiny new toy." In a world of constant technological innovations, thought leadership, and social media, it is so incredibly easy to get sucked into the "shiny new toy" – what's trendy, what everyone else is doing, and what's new and cool.

But, sometimes going against the status quo actually means getting back to basics and remembering that true leadership and great HR is simply about intention.

You must care enough to address the root of the issues rather than simply checking a box, to do the right thing rather than the popular thing, and to speak up versus worrying about making everyone happy.

It is critical to remember that leadership and HR are team sports, though. Thus, hiring differently is also a differentiator in leadership. We need to build a team of people who compliment us and others on our team rather than people who are exactly the same as us. Similarity bias is real, and it is plaguing workplaces across the world. We should be leading the way in diversifying with our HR teams before we can support the rest of the company to do this.

Feedback and Conflict

The third piece of the framework is about seeking out, providing, and embracing productive and unknown feedback, perspectives, and conflict. Without this, the gap in knowledge and experience is much wider.

Intentional leaders and HR departments live in feedback and conflict. We do not subscribe to the infamous sandwich feedback where we give a piece of positive feedback, sandwich some negative feedback in between, and then pile another compliment on top. We give feedback in a timely, productive, and helpful manner.

This was something that took me some time to learn myself. Intentional leaders offer feedback purposefully to support team members and build trust, which is the foundation. When we have trust, feedback is received as something that is believed to help us. It's also an ongoing, two-way dialogue. It's not just telling someone what's wrong with them and walking away.

Intentional leaders also manage conflict immediately so that it does not become a distraction. We practice the skills of facilitation, expectation-setting, and supporting team members to resolve issues together.

Not every solution will be the right solution for everyone, because, well, one size does not fit all. That means we must customize and personalize HR, and our leadership of it, to each person.

Personalization and Customization

This is about making each person feel like they belong and make it clear that their differences are embraced, rather than seen as problematic. However, this does not mean that intentional leaders and HR professionals do not make tough decisions about their teams. In fact, we are the ones who are best equipped to make difficult and/or unpopular decisions.

Similar to product management, we think about personalization as the push and customization as the pull. Personalizing leadership is understanding our teams' and our team members' needs and ensuring that we are designing the right environment to nurture those needs. Customization is about being open to what we do not know and being flexible and agile enough to allow our team members to pull from us what they need.

I used to set up weekly 1:1s with each team member early in my formal leadership career. One time, an employee told me, "I kind of feel like having our 1:1 weekly is a waste of my time and yours. I work very independently and prefer to put an ad hoc meeting on your calendar when I need something rather than waiting for a 1:1. Plus, as an HR Business Partner, I have a lot of meetings already and it would be nice to have more time to focus on my work without constantly working into the evenings."

I've always received the advice to meet with my teams regularly, to have 1:1s on a frequent recurring schedule. That's the advice our HR department was giving to leaders across the company too. That's how we lead, right? Well, as I came to realize, thanks to this frank and honest advice, it's not.

This is just one example of how we, as leaders and HR professionals, just adhere to "best practice" advice that may not actually be *good* practice. Perhaps, the best practice worked once upon a time, but now it is outdated. Or, perhaps, the best practice worked for a very specific situation and was unnecessarily applied to *all* situations. Thus, that best practice was actually unhelpful.

Ever since receiving this feedback, I've had an open dialogue with new team members to understand how they work best and how often we should meet. It's different for everyone and I have learned to be okay with that. And you know what? It has worked beautifully. We need to stop putting people into boxes and forcing them to operate "our" way or the same way, as we are used to or comfortable with.

Balanced Approach

The very last piece to the intentional HR leadership puzzle is a balanced approach. As a Libra, I'm all about balance and when I think about having a balanced leadership approach, improv comedy comes to mind. One of the most popular skills we get trained in for improv is "yes, and," which is the opposite of what we, as humans, tend to do when we do not agree with something, which is to respond with "no, but" or "but, no."

A "yes, and" approach allows us to bring people together, build understanding, make better decisions, and do the right thing. It is about building upon things rather than tearing things down and doing it our way. This is honestly how we will create meaningful and positive change.

I recall being a newer leader early in my career and receiving feedback that one of my new team members was not a good fit for the team. I was told that they were twiddling their thumbs, looking at their phone, and not paying attention during orientation.

I observed for myself. I saw the twiddling of the thumbs and the usage of the phone. You know what else I saw? Someone who finished their exercises nearly 20 minutes before everyone else, who won every trivia game on the content being trained, and who was not being challenged. They were *bored*. However, I didn't want to jump to conclusions, so I talked to them.

I shared what others observed, shared what I observed, and asked them to share their experience. Sure enough, they were bored out of their mind, so I worked to include optional advanced exercises into the orientation and gave this person some early responsibilities for the team. They turned out to be an incredibly valued team member who was not only promoted on my team but was eventually promoted by the same people who gave the original feedback after I had eventually moved on from the company. In fact, they eventually took on one of my previous roles after I left the team.

Now, I was not working in HR at the time, but we can only imagine if my peers and superiors went to HR instead of talking to me first. Would my employee have been fired? Would the outcome have been the same? Would I have had the opportunity to show everyone another perspective? Would I have had the opportunity to provide my team member the support they needed to succeed?

Sometimes, two seemingly opposing things can be true. *Yes*, my team member was showing behaviors stereotypically aligned with a disengaged employee, *and* that same team member was ready to learn more than what was being taught at the time of their orientation and were more than ready for more challenging work.

To come full circle, this is why a balanced approach in HR is necessary and why we must embrace a culture of autonomy where the people closest to the work are part of decisions that impact them and their teams.

Tiffany Castagno, the CEO of CEPHR and HR/Culture extraordinaire, recalls being an HR Business Partner (HRBP) and facing a tough employee relations situation. Not only were there compliance issues involved, but there were also team dynamics and interpersonal issues that presented themselves. A manager had concerns about an employee abusing their intermittent leave. From their perspective, the employee was frustrated that they didn't feel heard by their manager and that there was constant micromanagement of the time off they were taking to care for themselves and a family member. The employee and manager both expressed frustrations with the previous HRBP and not feeling supported by them.

As the HR professional in this situation, both the employee and the manager were looking to Tiffany to solve their issues, but Tiffany knew that this would require the involvement of all parties. She recognized that there was healing and repair that needed to happen. So, she supported both team members to understand, clarify, and work through the leave pieces and helped them understand what the other party involved needed.

More importantly, Tiffany made sure that all parties understood the part they played in resolution. She was there to provide coaching, guidance, and facilitation; but, ultimately, the manager and the employee had big roles to play in rebuilding their working relationship with each other. Tiffany offered the appropriate tools and resources they would need for resolution, and then she allowed the two to use those as they saw fit to resolve their issues. She also expressed her belief, confidence, and trust in their ability to resolve their issues *together*.

She didn't make assumptions about what the perfect solution would be for them. She didn't demand that they go a certain direction. She knew what she could and should offer and when to step aside to allow others closest to the situation to do what they needed to do. Ultimately, there was a happy ending, and the team was able to work through their concerns; as well as the unhealthy triangulation issue between the employee, manager, and HR. [1]

In order to impact culture, we must build trust. In order to build trust, we must get out of the way, support and allow people to lead and do their work, and share in the accountability for what the company or organization lives and breathes. We *must* be more *intentional*.

---

1. Tiffany Costagno [Interview]. 2 January 2024

Conclusion

THERE WILL ALWAYS be pandemics, emergencies, recessions, social unrest, and so much more that will impact and disrupt our businesses. I really believe that the only way through these challenging times is great HR and great leadership. As I advanced in my career, I came to realize that great HR and great leadership go hand-in-hand. Great HR teams empower great leaders across the company and great leaders empower strategic and meaningful HR programs. They *fuel* each other.

Throughout my career, I've had the opportunity to learn from and work with some incredible operational leaders in finance, IT, marketing, and more. I even learned more from a finance peer about budgeting, income statements, and revenue forecasting than I ever learned in my college finance classes. I learned to code and build a website from a peer in IT. I dramatically improved my written and verbal communication skills just by working with a peer in marketing. In turn, they have shared with me how they have grown and developed as leaders through their work with my team and me.

Paul, our HR Philosopher from Chapter 1, also shared about how he has learned from industry leaders both internally and externally throughout his career that even led him to obtaining a non-HR certification. He felt this helped him understand his organization's mission and the greater industry much better, which in turn, supported him in being a more effective HR leader.

To achieve that ideal harmony between HR and the rest of the company, we must remember the tenets that we learned in the last five chapters. There is a printable infographic that summarizes these and it is available via the link at the back of the book.

- Get out of HR and our offices to experience the joy of learning the business and building relationships.

- Get out of our own heads to experience the joy of solving real problems that make a difference.

- Get out of our assumptions to experience the joy of communicating effectively and supporting others to do the same.

- Get out of our comfort zones to experience the joy of doing the right thing.

- Get out of the way and get intentional to experience the joy of impacting culture in a meaningful way.

- We *must* get out of the way and get intentional to experience the joy of impacting culture in a meaningful way.

There will always be obstacles or issues in our profession that challenge our desire to stay in it. Because it is, in many respects, a very demanding job. We are often asked to take on extra work with very little reward, expected to balance all the various and conflicting needs of our people with grace, and pressured to carry the weight of company culture on our shoulders. We deal with some heavy things in HR and it can sometimes take the joy out of it for us. This weight certainly takes a toll.

My hope for all of us is that we can channel our inner Steve Browne and center ourselves in the joy of it all. Finding creative and intentional ways to overcome the challenges of our industry can help us discover, or rediscover, the joys with the people and HR industry in this new world of work that we're in.

The five principles of this book will allow us, as HR professionals, to really experience and share in the joy of HR. Because yes, HR really *can* be a *joy* – to work with and to be a part of.

Keep the Joy Going

Congratulations, you've completed the book! Don't stop the learning process though. Keep the joy going by taking advantage of our free resources for readers. Scan the QR code or visit www.talentmix.com/bookresources/.

Here's what you'll get:

The Five Tenets

Download and print or save the five tenets so you always have a quick refresher, or use it to support your teams or leaders.

Intentional Leadership Framework

Print and hang it up or save it in an easy-to-access digital space so you can refer to it often and hold yourself and your leaders accountable for exercising great intention.

Discussion Questions

Explore thought-provoking questions for your book club, reading group, leadership development audience, company or team retreat, or personal growth.

Make A Greater Impact Infographic

Keep this reminder from Chapter 1 of the list of ways to "get out of HR" to build stronger relationships and make a bigger impact. This is a non-exhaustive but comprehensive list.

Newsletter

Stay up on all the latest and greatest thoughts as it relates to leadership, HR, talent, DEIB, and startups.

Send us your questions and they might just get answered in the newsletter!

Acknowledgements

Even the thought of writing a book was daunting for me. Committing to my first book was terrifying. Actually writing my first book was as challenging as I expected but much more rewarding than I could have ever anticipated.

None of this would have been possible without my incredible community. It's amazing how every stage in life brings new people into your life who change it forever. Who knew writing a book would be considered an entire stage of life for me?!

Above all, I am eternally grateful to my family. My spouse, Jordan, has and always will be my rock. His constant and genuine belief in me and my ability to finish this book was so critical in motivating me during the hard times. He lifted me up through the darkest moments, celebrated with me during the brightest ones, and cheered me on all along the way. His unwavering love and support have been my safe and happy place throughout this entire experience, as it is throughout life.

I would be remiss not to thank the joys of my life who have given me the best role in the world, mom. Lil Buck and Baby Buck are my everyday reminder that no matter how hard life, or writing this book, gets, I will still have lifelong joy and a full heart because I have them. They are my "why" and along with their father, the loves of my life. There is nothing in the world I am more appreciative of than them. When I told Lil Buck I was writing a book, she immediately decided to write one too, and it was quite good. She finished hers in only a few days and really showed me up – she really is the best inspiration, motivation, and accountability partner.

When I committed to writing this book, I had to select a publisher, editor, and designer. I knew these would be three crucial roles in this journey. Ultimately, I partnered with INM as my publisher because of a recommendation from a friend and colleague. I'm happy to say that I have no regrets. I'm honored that Melanie Booher reached out to me and I thank her for her confidence in me ever since we met. Working with Jodi Brandstetter as my book coach has been a wonderful experience. Jodi is patient, generous, and experienced. She held me accountable, kept me on track, talked me out of my own head several times, and really supported me throughout the entire process. As someone who is flawed with impatience and was writing a book while raising two young kids and running a business, it was a dream to work with Jodi as she was highly responsive and flexible.

A big thank you, as well, to my editor, Alexandra (Alex) Glossner, for making sure that my voice shines throughout the book, but also that I made sense to others. I'm so glad we got to work on this together and am grateful for your guidance.

While selecting my publisher and editor was a little scary since I've never worked with one before, finding my designer could not have been easier. I immediately knew who I wanted to work with for my covers. Michell

Moy, my exceptionally talented designer, I am over the moon with how my covers turned out. Michell and I go back a long time to my corporate days, and it has been just as much of a privilege to work with her on this project as it was back in the day. Her ability to translate my chaotic thoughts into a beautiful and meaningful design is second to none.

The mission of giving back and supporting future generations of business leaders was top of mind for me as I wrote the book; so I am eternally grateful for all my seriously inspiring and brilliant peers in the industry who agreed to be a part of the book.

First, I could not be more honored to have a Foreword from the LEGEND, Steve Browne – you are a true gift to everyone in the #HRCommunity and I'll never know how you do it all, but I am grateful that you do. Thank you for being you and thank you for being in my corner and sharing your storytelling gift with the world through the beautifully joyful Foreword you wrote.

Tiffany Castagno, Sarika Lamont, Cat Colella-Graham, and Paul LaLonde – thank you for blessing us all with your honest, uplifting, and impactful stories. I know that they will resonate with people and help them. It means the world to me to have you as such a critical part of this journey.

Laura Ladd – thank you for allowing me to share your story in my own words and from my front row seat where I got to see you thrive and make places and spaces better than when you found them.

Gregory Tall, Jeanan Yasiri Moe, Andrew Higashi, Enrique Rubio, JoAnn Corley, Joni Duncan, TJ Mercer, Allison Lackey Peschel, Emily Endert, and Raphi Savitz – thank you for being an integral part of my book and for sharing your love with me and with my audience. I admire each one of you more than words can express and am full of immense gratitude for your generosity and ongoing support.

To my #HRCommunity – thank you for continuing to inspire me and teach me new things. I am constantly learning from you all and you help me be a better HR professional, leader, and person. Nothing but love to you all!

To my greater community – my family, my friends, my colleagues, my fellow volunteers, my fellow Illini and Gies College of Business alumni network, my Badger network, and more – I do think it matters who you surround yourself with and I am so appreciative that I get to surround myself with all of you. I love you!

About the Author

Lotus Buckner is a seasoned People & Culture (HR) leader, recognized for her people-centric, strategic executive expertise. As a startup advisor, entrepreneur, speaker, and consultant, she leverages her diverse experience to guide companies throughout the employee lifecycle, aligning their people and business strategies with exceptional results. Buckner is also an accomplished coach; working with founders, executives, and senior leaders to elevate their leadership, careers, and companies.

With a track record of acclaim from organizations like Crain's Chicago Business, Buckner shares her insights globally, speaking for a range of organizations and associations. Including Guaranteed Rate, ACHE, and DePaul University SHRM. She's a published writer in prestigious outlets like Forbes and a sought-after speaker and podcast guest.

Buckner's expertise spans various HR and business topics. Including business strategy, leadership alignment, DEIB, employee experience, talent development, HR programs, and career growth. Whether through speaking engagements, consultations, advisory services, fractional work, coaching, or content development, Buckner can bring substantial value to you and your organization.

About Talent Remix

At **Talent Remix**, we offer coaching, advisory, and speaking services designed to elevate leadership capabilities for organizations and individuals. Our comprehensive suite of offerings also includes fractional, interim, and consulting services to transform and advance HR, People, and Talent teams into robust business functions and strategic partners.

We're on a mission to level the playing field at work by creating a learning ecosystem that supports professionals and businesses. Through our dynamic services, we bring out the best in you and your talented teams. We've delivered impactful sessions on:

- Leadership
- Strategic planning

- Diversity, Equity, Inclusion, Belonging+ (DEIB+)

- Internal Communications

- Employee experience

- Business Alignment

- Executive Development

While we serve a variety of clients, we focus heavily on senior leaders, executive teams, CEOs, founders, and HR/People/Talent/DEIB teams.

Discover how Talent Remix can support your company's goals and help you achieve excellence. Visit www.talentremix.com.

Printed in the USA
CPSIA information can be obtained
at www.ICGtesting.com
CBHW070139150824
13129CB00055B/588